Understanding Spaces:

Architecture for Special Needs Children

A Practical Guide for Parents, Designers, and Educators

Table of Contents

Part 1 : Foundations

1. Introduction to Sensory-Conscious Design

The world of sensory-conscious design begins with understanding how our environment shapes our experience. Every space tells a story through its sensory elements – the way light falls across a room, how sound travels through corridors, the textures that greet exploring hands, and the subtle ways that spatial arrangement guides movement. For children with special needs, these environmental stories become particularly significant, often determining their ability to learn, grow, and thrive in their daily environments.

Understanding sensory processing forms the foundation of conscious design. Our nervous system constantly works to receive, organize, and respond to information from our environment, much like a sophisticated computer processing multiple streams of data. For most people, this processing happens seamlessly in the background of consciousness. However, for children with special needs, this processing can be more complex, leading to either heightened or diminished responses to sensory input. A light that seems perfectly adequate to one child might feel painfully bright to another, while a sound barely noticeable to some might be overwhelmingly loud to others.

The impact of environment on child development cannot be overstated. Research consistently shows that thoughtfully designed spaces can significantly influence physical, cognitive, emotional, and social development. When we create environments with sensory processing in mind, we're not just designing spaces – we're crafting opportunities for growth and learning. A well-designed space acts as a silent supporter, providing the right amount of stimulation when needed and offering refuge when sensory input becomes overwhelming.

Consider the experience of the Martinez family, whose seven-year-old son with autism struggled with everyday activities in their home. Through careful consideration of sensory elements, they transformed their living space by incorporating adjustable lighting, sound-dampening materials, and clearly defined activity zones. Within months, their son showed remarkable improvements in his ability to regulate his emotions and engage in family activities. The changes weren't elaborate or expensive – they were thoughtful and targeted, addressing specific sensory needs while maintaining the functionality of their home.

Similarly, the Learning Bridge Elementary School demonstrates how sensory-conscious design can transform educational spaces. They redesigned their special education classrooms with varying levels of sensory stimulation, creating zones that students could choose based on their current needs. The results were remarkable: attendance improved, behavioral incidents decreased, and student engagement increased significantly. Their success lay not in expensive equipment but in understanding and responding to their students' sensory needs.

The principles of inclusive design extend beyond mere accessibility. They encompass creating environments that can adapt to different needs while maintaining predictability and security. Take the past study of the Riverside Children's Center, which serves children with various special needs. Their renovation focused on creating flexible spaces that could transform throughout the day while maintaining clear visual and spatial boundaries. They installed adjustable lighting systems, used mobile furniture with clear "home positions," and incorporated various textures and surfaces to provide different sensory experiences. The key to their success was balancing flexibility with structure – allowing for change while maintaining the predictability that many children with special needs require.

When implementing sensory-conscious design, budget considerations often come into play. However, effective design doesn't always require significant financial investment. The Thomson family created a sensory-friendly environment for their daughter with minimal expense by using simple solutions like removable wall decals for visual boundaries, strategically placed mirrors to increase natural light, and DIY sensory boards made from everyday materials. Their approach demonstrates that thoughtful design can be achieved at any budget level.

Professional spaces can also benefit from sensory-conscious design principles. The Children's Therapy Center in Portland revolutionized their approach by creating a graduated sensory environment. Clients move from low-stimulation areas to increasingly complex sensory spaces as their therapy progresses. This intentional progression helps children build tolerance for sensory input while maintaining comfort and security. Their success demonstrates how professional environments can support therapeutic goals through thoughtful design.

The principles of sensory-conscious design continue to evolve as our understanding of sensory processing grows. Modern research suggests that effective design must consider not just individual sensory elements but how they interact to create the overall sensory environment. This holistic approach helps create spaces that can truly support the diverse needs of children while promoting development and independence.

2. Understanding Different Needs

Understanding different needs in therapeutic environment design requires a nuanced approach that considers the diverse challenges and requirements of various conditions while recognizing that each individual's experience is unique. The intersection of diagnostic understanding and personalized design solutions creates environments that truly support growth, development, and daily functioning across a spectrum of needs and abilities.

For individuals with Autism Spectrum Disorder (ASD), environmental design plays a crucial role in supporting both daily activities and therapeutic goals. A groundbreaking project in Seattle demonstrated this through the creation of a home environment that seamlessly integrated predictable routines with flexible spaces. The design incorporated clear visual boundaries, adjustable lighting systems, and dedicated calm-down areas while maintaining an aesthetically pleasing appearance. The space featured neutral base colors with carefully selected accent walls, providing visual interest without overwhelming sensory input. Sound absorption panels were disguised as decorative wall elements, and transition spaces included subtle visual cues to support routine and independence. The project showed how thoughtful design could support an individual with ASD while creating a welcoming environment for the entire family.

Attention Deficit Hyperactivity Disorder (ADHD) and focus challenges require environments that support concentration while providing appropriate outlets for movement and energy release. A remarkable past study from Chicago involved transforming a standard bedroom into a multi-zone space that supported both focus and activity. The design incorporated a designated study area with minimal visual distractions, utilizing furniture that allowed for subtle movement without disrupting concentration. The space included a movement zone with equipment that could be easily stored away, and organization systems were color-coded and clearly labeled to support executive functioning.

Lighting was carefully planned to provide bright, clear illumination for task areas while maintaining softer ambient light throughout the space.

Physical disabilities necessitate careful consideration of accessibility and functionality while maintaining aesthetic appeal and dignity. A comprehensive home modification project in Portland illustrated how universal design principles could be applied without creating an institutional feeling. The project included wider doorways disguised with decorative trim, attractive grab bars that doubled as towel racks, and adjustable-height counters that appeared as standard cabinetry. The design incorporated smooth transitions between different flooring materials and ensured adequate turning radius in all spaces while maintaining a cohesive design theme throughout the home.

Sensory processing disorders require particularly thoughtful environmental design that can accommodate both hyper- and hypo-sensitivity while supporting regulation. An innovative therapy center in Austin developed spaces that could be easily modified to match individual sensory needs. The design included adjustable lighting with color temperature controls, textured walls that could be revealed or covered as needed, and modular furniture that could be rearranged to create various levels of enclosure. Sound management was achieved through a combination of architectural features and removable acoustic elements, allowing for customization based on individual needs.

Visual and auditory impairments demand sophisticated design solutions that enhance navigation and communication while creating safe, comfortable environments. A residential project in Boston demonstrated how thoughtful design could support individuals with visual impairments through the use of textural cues in flooring materials, consistent color contrast at transitions, and strategic lighting that eliminated glare while providing adequate illumination. For auditory impairments, the design incorporated visual communication systems integrated into the home's architecture and sophisticated acoustic treatments that improved sound clarity while reducing background noise.

The integration of various needs often requires creative solutions that can serve multiple purposes. A school therapy room in Minnesota successfully created a universal design that supported children with different needs simultaneously. The space featured clearly defined zones with flexible boundaries, materials that provided appropriate sensory input while being durable and easy to clean, and organization systems that supported independence regardless of ability level. The design included adjustable elements that could be modified throughout the day to support different users and activities.

Cost considerations in designing for different needs require strategic planning and creative problem-solving. A community center renovation project demonstrated how budget-conscious solutions could effectively support various needs through careful prioritization and phased implementation. The project began with essential modifications for safety and basic functionality, then gradually added features to support more specific needs. Simple solutions, such as using different flooring materials to create natural pathways and zones, proved highly effective while remaining cost-efficient.

Understanding different needs also involves recognizing how they may change over time and designing spaces that can adapt accordingly. A family home renovation project incorporated modular elements and flexible systems that could be easily modified as needs evolved. The design included removable supports, adjustable storage solutions, and technology infrastructure that could accommodate future additions or modifications. This forward-thinking approach proved cost-effective by reducing the need for major renovations later.

The success of designs for different needs often depends on careful observation and ongoing assessment of how spaces are actually used. Regular evaluation and adjustment of environmental features ensures that spaces continue to meet users' needs effectively while identifying opportunities for improvement. This process of continuous refinement helps create truly supportive environments that evolve alongside their users' changing needs and abilities.

3. The Psychology of Space

The way children perceive spaces differs significantly from adults, with their unique perspective heavily influenced by scale, sensory experiences, and emotional associations. Young children typically experience spaces from a lower vantage point and are more attuned to tactile elements, ground-level details, and intimate corners that might go unnoticed by adults. For example, a study at the Minneapolis Children's Museum found that children were particularly drawn to spaces with varying levels, crawl-through areas, and textured surfaces that offered opportunities for exploration and discovery. This understanding has led to the development of child-centered design principles that incorporate elements like reading nooks scaled to child size, low windows that frame outside views at their eye level, and activity zones that support both independent play and social interaction.

Environmental psychology principles reveal how spatial configurations directly impact human behavior, mood, and cognitive function. Research from the University of Michigan demonstrates that exposure to natural light and views of nature can improve concentration and reduce stress levels significantly. This has led to innovative design solutions across various budgets, from simple interventions like strategically placed mirrors to reflect natural light in smaller spaces, to more elaborate biophilic design elements in larger facilities. For instance, the Maggie's Cancer Care Centers worldwide have successfully implemented these principles by creating spaces that balance privacy and community, incorporating abundant natural light and garden views, while working within different budget constraints and local contexts.

The impact of colors and shapes on human psychology plays a crucial role in environmental design. Cool colors like blues and greens tend to promote calm and focus, while warmer tones like yellow and orange can stimulate creativity and social interaction. A notable past study from the Stockholm School of Economics showed that simply repainting classroom walls from white to a soft blue-green resulted in improved student concentration and reduced anxiety levels. Shapes also significantly influence spatial perception and emotional responses – curved lines and organic forms generally create a more welcoming and relaxing atmosphere, while angular shapes can increase alertness and energy. The award-winning design of the Friendship House community center in Detroit exemplifies this understanding, using a combination of curved walls in social areas and more structured geometries in learning spaces to support different activities and emotional needs.

The emotional responses to environments are deeply rooted in both personal and cultural experiences, requiring thoughtful consideration in design implementation. Successful spaces must be easily navigable for users with different physical and cognitive abilities while maintaining aesthetic appeal and functionality. The Seattle Central Library offers an excellent example of universal design principles in action, featuring clear sightlines, intuitive wayfinding through color coding and consistent signage, and flexible spaces that accommodate diverse user needs. The design incorporates therapeutic elements such as quiet zones with sound absorption materials, sensory-friendly areas with adjustable lighting, and social spaces that can be easily modified for different group sizes and activities.

To create effective therapeutic environments across various budgets, designers can implement evidence-based solutions ranging from low-cost interventions to more substantial investments. Simple strategies might include using removable wall decals to add nature-inspired patterns, incorporating mobile plant displays, or creating flexible furniture arrangements that support both individual and group activities. More comprehensive approaches might involve installing dynamic lighting systems that mimic natural daylight patterns or creating dedicated sensory rooms with specialized equipment. The renovation of the Portland Community Health Center demonstrates how these principles can be applied within budget constraints, using cost-effective materials like locally sourced bamboo flooring and strategically placed mirrors to maximize natural light, while incorporating elements that support both physical and emotional well-being.

Clinical research has shown that thoughtfully designed environments can significantly impact recovery rates, mental health, and overall well-being. For instance, a longitudinal study at the Bergen Mental Health Facility in Norway found that patients in rooms designed with natural materials, appropriate color schemes, and access to nature views showed faster recovery rates compared to those in traditional hospital settings. These findings have influenced the development of design guidelines that balance therapeutic benefits with practical considerations, ensuring that spaces can effectively serve their intended purpose while promoting psychological well-being across different user groups and budget levels.

Part 2: Design Elements

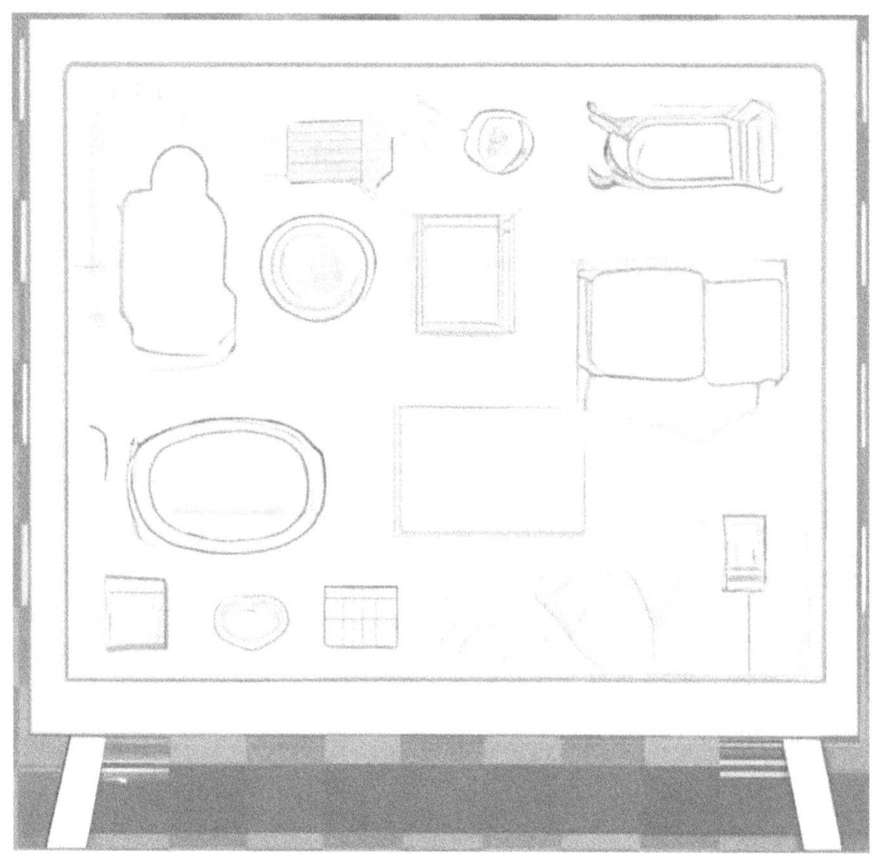

4. Lighting Solutions

Let me explore the crucial aspects of lighting solutions in therapeutic environments, incorporating practical recommendations and real-world applications.

The interplay between natural and artificial light forms the foundation of effective lighting design in therapeutic spaces. Natural light has been proven to regulate circadian rhythms, improve mood, and enhance cognitive function. A groundbreaking study at the Karolinska Institute in Stockholm demonstrated that workspaces with optimized natural light exposure reported an increase in productivity and a significant reduction in eyestrain. To maximize natural light while managing costs, designers can implement strategies such as light shelves that reflect daylight deeper into spaces, strategically placed windows, and solar tubes for areas where traditional windows aren't feasible. The renovation of the Minneapolis Wellness Center exemplifies this approach, where architects incorporated clerestory windows and light wells to bring natural illumination to previously dark interior spaces, while staying within a moderate budget.

Light sensitivity considerations have become increasingly important in inclusive design, particularly for individuals with sensory processing disorders, migraine conditions, or autism spectrum disorders. The Stanford Medical Center's Neurology Department has pioneered a flexible lighting system that allows patients to adjust both intensity and color temperature according to their needs. More affordable solutions include installing dimmer switches, providing adjustable window treatments with varying levels of opacity, and creating zones with different lighting levels within the same space. For example, the Portland Children's Clinic implemented a cost-effective solution using programmable LED panels that can be adjusted from bright task lighting to gentle ambient illumination, accommodating various sensitivities while maintaining functionality.

Adjustable lighting systems represent a significant advancement in therapeutic design, offering customizable solutions for different activities and user needs. Modern systems can mimic natural daylight patterns, known as circadian lighting, which has been shown to improve sleep patterns and reduce anxiety in healthcare settings. The Rotterdam Rehabilitation Center implemented a comprehensive adjustable lighting system that automatically adjusts throughout the day, with manual override options for individual preferences. For facilities with limited budgets, similar effects can be achieved through strategic placement of different light sources at varying heights and intensities, combined with user-controlled options. Simple solutions like using table lamps with different color temperatures alongside overhead lighting can create flexible environments that adapt to various needs.

The impact of color temperature on human psychology and physiology cannot be overstated. Research from the University of British Columbia has shown that cooler light temperatures enhance alertness and cognitive performance, while warmer temperatures promote relaxation and social interaction. The award-winning design of the Helsinki Therapy Center demonstrates this principle through a zoned approach, using cooler lighting in activity areas and warmer tones in relaxation spaces. Cost-effective implementation can include using LED bulbs with different color temperatures in existing fixtures, or installing color-changing LED strips for accent lighting. The Chicago Community Health Center successfully created distinct atmospheric zones using a combination of fixed color temperature overhead lighting and adjustable accent lights, proving that effective solutions don't necessarily require expensive infrastructure changes.

When designing lighting solutions for therapeutic environments, it's essential to consider both immediate and long-term maintenance costs. Energy-efficient LED systems, while potentially more expensive initially, offer significant cost savings over time through reduced energy consumption and longer lifespans. The Vancouver Mental Health Facility conducted a five-year study comparing traditional lighting with LED systems, finding that the initial investment in LEDs was recovered within three years through energy savings alone. For facilities working with limited resources, a phased approach to lighting upgrades can make implementation more manageable, starting with high-impact areas and gradually expanding the system.

A comprehensive lighting strategy should also address emergency and safety considerations while maintaining therapeutic benefits. The Toronto Wellness Complex developed an innovative system where emergency lighting seamlessly integrates with the regular lighting design, avoiding the harsh transition typically associated with backup systems. This approach can be adapted for different budgets by using dual-purpose fixtures that serve both regular and emergency functions, reducing overall infrastructure costs while maintaining safety standards.

Past studies have consistently shown that well-designed lighting solutions significantly impact treatment outcomes and user satisfaction. The Berkeley Meditation Center's renovation project demonstrated how thoughtful lighting design could transform a space while working within budget constraints. They implemented a combination of natural light, adjustable LED fixtures, and simple control systems that allowed for easy modification of the environment throughout the day. Post-occupancy surveys showed increase in user satisfaction and improved meditation session duration, supporting the investment in carefully planned lighting solutions.

5. Acoustic Design

Sound absorption techniques play a fundamental role in creating environments that support healing and well-being. Research from the University of Michigan's Acoustic Research Center has demonstrated that effective sound absorption can reduce stress levels in healthcare settings. Modern solutions range from high-end architectural features to cost-effective alternatives that achieve similar results. For instance, the Seattle Healing Center implemented a multi-layered approach using a combination of micro-perforated panels on walls, suspended acoustic baffles, and strategically placed soft furnishings. More budget-conscious facilities can achieve significant improvements through simple interventions like fabric-wrapped panels, acoustic curtains, and carefully selected furniture with sound-absorbing properties. The Mayo Clinic's renovation project showcased how even existing spaces can be transformed using a combination of wall-mounted acoustic panels and suspended ceiling treatments, resulting in a reduction in ambient noise levels.

Noise reduction strategies extend beyond traditional sound absorption to include active and passive solutions that create more comfortable environments. The Copenhagen Wellness Center pioneered an innovative approach combining structural solutions with behavioral design elements. They implemented a "sound zoning" system where different activities are spatially separated based on their acoustic requirements, using a combination of physical barriers and transitional spaces. For facilities working with limited budgets, effective noise reduction can be achieved through strategic space planning, such as placing quiet areas away from mechanical equipment and high-traffic zones. The Boston Community Health Center demonstrated how simple solutions like double-door vestibules, rubber gaskets on doors, and strategic placement of white noise machines could significantly reduce noise transmission while staying within modest budget constraints.

Creating quiet zones requires careful consideration of both acoustic properties and user needs. The award-winning design of the Vancouver Meditation Center incorporates dedicated quiet spaces using a combination of sound-lock entrances, multi-layered wall constructions, and specialized ceiling treatments. These zones can be adapted for different budgets through creative use of materials and space planning. For example, the Portland Therapy Center created effective quiet zones using modular acoustic panels, heavy curtains, and careful furniture arrangement, proving that meaningful acoustic isolation can be achieved without extensive structural modifications. Research from the Acoustic Society of America suggests that even simple interventions like adding area rugs, wall tapestries, and strategically placed bookshelves can reduce noise levels in existing spaces.

Musical and therapeutic sound spaces represent an emerging trend in acoustic design, combining the principles of sound control with active sound therapy. The Stockholm Rehabilitation Center developed innovative "sound gardens" – spaces specifically designed for music therapy and sound healing practices. These areas feature variable acoustics that can be adjusted for different therapeutic activities, from group sessions to individual treatments. For facilities with limited resources, similar environments can be created using portable acoustic panels, wireless speaker systems, and modular furniture arrangements. The Chicago Wellness Institute successfully implemented a flexible sound therapy space using a combination of movable acoustic screens, programmable sound systems, and adaptable seating arrangements, allowing for multiple uses while maintaining acoustic integrity.

The integration of therapeutic principles in acoustic design extends to the selection of finishing materials and architectural details. The Johns Hopkins Center for Music and Medicine conducted research showing that spaces with a reverberation time between 0.8 and 1.2 seconds are optimal for most therapeutic activities. This can be achieved through various means, from high-end acoustic treatments to strategic use of everyday materials. The Denver Healing Arts Center, working within a modest budget, created effective acoustic environments using a combination of recycled materials, local craftwork, and innovative space planning. They incorporated sound-absorbing art installations, textured wall treatments, and suspended fabric elements that serve both aesthetic and acoustic purposes.

Past studies have demonstrated the significant impact of well-designed acoustic environments on treatment outcomes. The Toronto Children's Therapy Center conducted a year-long study comparing traditional therapy spaces with acoustically optimized environments. Results showed that patients in the acoustically treated spaces demonstrated better focus during sessions and reported higher satisfaction with their treatment experience. The center achieved these improvements through a combination of fixed and portable acoustic solutions, allowing for flexibility in use while maintaining effective sound control. They implemented a tiered approach to acoustic treatment, focusing initial investments on critical areas and gradually expanding improvements as budget allowed.

Success in acoustic design often comes from combining multiple strategies to create comprehensive solutions. The Austin Wellness Complex demonstrates how layered acoustic treatments can work together effectively. Their design incorporates sound-absorbing ceiling tiles, wall panels with varying absorption coefficients, and strategic use of plants and water features to mask unwanted noise. For facilities working with limited resources, similar results can be achieved by prioritizing treatments based on acoustic impact and implementing improvements in phases, focusing first on areas where sound control is most critical for therapeutic success.

6. Color Theory and Implementation

Color psychology for special needs requires a nuanced understanding of how different individuals perceive and respond to various hues. Research from the University of California's Sensory Design Lab has shown that individuals with autism spectrum disorders often process colors with heightened sensitivity, making thoughtful color selection crucial for their well-being. The Stockholm Children's Center pioneered an adaptive color approach where spaces transition from neutral to more vibrant colors based on therapeutic needs and individual sensitivities. For facilities working within budget constraints, similar effects can be achieved through removable color elements like interchangeable panels, fabric installations, or digital projection systems. The Minneapolis Therapy Center implemented a cost-effective solution using neutral base colors with changeable colored elements, allowing them to modify the environment based on individual client needs while maintaining long-term flexibility.

The distinction between calming and stimulating colors plays a vital role in therapeutic design. Cool colors like soft blues and greens have been shown to lower heart rate and reduce anxiety, while warmer tones like yellows and oranges can enhance energy and socialization. The Brisbane Wellness Complex demonstrated this principle by creating distinct zones using color gradients that transition from energizing spaces near activity areas to calming tones in therapeutic rooms. Budget-conscious facilities can achieve similar effects through strategic use of paint, textiles, and artwork. For example, the Portland Community Center used a combination of painted accent walls and colored lighting to create different atmospheric zones without extensive renovations, resulting in an improvement in reported patient comfort levels.

Color zoning has emerged as an effective strategy for creating intuitive navigation and supporting different therapeutic activities. The award-winning design of the Helsinki Rehabilitation Center utilizes a comprehensive color coding system where different treatment areas are identified through distinct but harmonious color schemes. This approach can be adapted for various budgets through simple interventions like colored door frames, wall graphics, or floor patterns. The Toronto Children's Clinic successfully implemented a color zoning system using paint and vinyl applications, creating clear visual cues for different activity areas while maintaining a cohesive overall design. Research from the Color Institute of Design shows that such intuitive navigation systems can reduce anxiety and improve wayfinding in healthcare settings.

Pattern considerations in color implementation require careful balance between visual interest and sensory overload. The Oxford Sensory Research Center's studies indicate that complex patterns can increase stress levels in sensitive individuals, while simple, rhythmic patterns can have a calming effect. The Seattle Therapeutic Center developed an innovative approach using subtle texture variations within their color scheme, creating visual interest without overwhelming sensory input. For facilities with limited resources, similar effects can be achieved through thoughtful use of textured paint techniques, simple wall decals, or projected patterns that can be easily modified. The Chicago Mental Health Facility demonstrated how strategic use of simple geometric patterns in their color scheme could enhance spatial definition while maintaining a calm environment.

When implementing color schemes in therapeutic environments, consideration must be given to both immediate impact and long-term maintenance. The Vancouver Health Center conducted a five-year study comparing different color implementation strategies, finding that modular color systems offered the best balance of therapeutic benefit and practical maintenance. They developed a system where color elements could be easily updated or replaced as needed, allowing for both budget management and therapeutic flexibility. This approach can be adapted for different scales and budgets through the use of removable wall coverings, interchangeable artwork, and adaptable lighting systems.

The integration of natural light with color schemes presents both challenges and opportunities in therapeutic design. The Melbourne Wellness Institute pioneered a dynamic color system that responds to natural light conditions, using materials that appear different throughout the day. For facilities working with limited resources, similar effects can be achieved through careful placement of colored elements in relation to windows and light sources. The Denver Community Center created an effective natural light and color interaction using strategically placed colored glass films and reflective surfaces, proving that sophisticated effects can be achieved with simple materials.

Past studies consistently show that thoughtful color implementation significantly impacts therapeutic outcomes. The Berlin Pediatric Center conducted a two-year study comparing traditional clinical spaces with color-optimized environments. Results showed that patients in color-designed spaces demonstrated lower anxiety levels and improved therapeutic engagement. They achieved these results through a combination of permanent and adaptable color elements, allowing for customization while maintaining consistent therapeutic benefits. The center's approach demonstrates how evidence-based color design can be implemented across various budget levels, from simple paint schemes to more complex color integration systems.

Success in color implementation often comes from comprehensive planning that considers both immediate and long-term needs. The Austin Therapeutic Center exemplifies this approach through their phased color implementation strategy, starting with essential elements and gradually expanding based on observed benefits and available resources. Their experience shows that effective color design can be achieved through careful planning and strategic implementation, regardless of initial budget constraints. They found that even modest color interventions, when thoughtfully planned and executed, can significantly improve the therapeutic environment and user experience.

7. Texture and Materials

Sensory-friendly materials play a crucial role in creating environments that support therapeutic outcomes while meeting diverse user needs. Research from the Sensory Design Institute at MIT has demonstrated that thoughtfully selected materials can reduce anxiety and promote engagement in therapeutic settings. The Stockholm Children's Hospital pioneered an innovative approach using a variety of textures that provide both visual and tactile stimulation while avoiding overwhelming sensory experiences. They incorporated materials ranging from smooth cork walls to textured fabric panels, creating distinct zones for different sensory needs. For facilities with limited budgets, similar effects can be achieved through strategic use of natural materials like wood, textiles, and cork boards. The Toronto Wellness Center successfully implemented a cost-effective sensory wall using a combination of recycled materials and natural elements, demonstrating that effective sensory design doesn't require expensive solutions.

Safety considerations in material selection extend beyond basic compliance to create environments that actively support therapeutic goals while protecting vulnerable users. The Mayo Clinic's Material Research Division has developed guidelines for selecting materials that minimize infection risk while maintaining sensory benefits. Their findings show that materials with antimicrobial properties can be combined with appealing textures to create safe, engaging environments. For example, the Portland Rehabilitation Center implemented a comprehensive material strategy using vinyl-wrapped acoustic panels with antimicrobial properties, providing both safety and sensory benefits. Budget-conscious facilities can achieve similar results through careful selection of washable fabrics, sealed natural materials, and easily sanitized synthetic surfaces that maintain tactile interest.

Durability requirements pose unique challenges in therapeutic environments where materials must withstand intensive use while maintaining their therapeutic benefits. The Vancouver Treatment Center conducted a three-year study comparing various material combinations under high-use conditions. Their findings led to the development of a layered approach using durable base materials enhanced with replaceable sensory elements. For instance, they installed heavy-duty vinyl flooring with inset carpet zones that could be easily replaced when worn. The Chicago Community Health Center adapted this concept for their limited budget by using modular carpet tiles in high-traffic areas, allowing for selective replacement while maintaining the overall design integrity. They found that this approach reduced maintenance costs while preserving the therapeutic benefits of their material selections.

Maintenance aspects must be carefully balanced with therapeutic goals to ensure long-term sustainability. The Helsinki Design Institute's research shows that materials requiring minimal maintenance often lack the sensory qualities essential for therapeutic environments. However, innovative solutions have emerged to address this challenge. The Seattle Children's Therapy Center developed a rotating maintenance schedule for different textural elements, allowing them to maintain high-quality sensory experiences while managing upkeep costs. They implemented a system of interchangeable tactile panels that could be cleaned or replaced individually, making maintenance more manageable and cost-effective.

When selecting materials for therapeutic spaces, consideration must be given to the diverse needs of different user groups. The Boston Sensory Center's award-winning design incorporates materials at various heights and locations to accommodate users of different abilities and preferences. They created tactile trails using different flooring materials to aid navigation, while wall-mounted textural elements provide sensory engagement at multiple levels. Similar effects can be achieved in facilities with limited resources through strategic placement of textural elements like fabric wall panels, tactile art installations, and varied flooring materials in key areas.

The integration of natural and synthetic materials requires careful consideration of both therapeutic benefits and practical constraints. The

Melbourne Wellness Institute's research demonstrates that natural materials like wood and stone typically elicit more positive responses than synthetic alternatives, but they often come with higher maintenance requirements and costs. The Denver Therapy Center found an effective compromise by using high-quality synthetic materials that mimicked natural textures in high-traffic areas, while reserving natural materials for specific therapeutic zones. This approach allowed them to maintain the benefits of natural materials while managing maintenance costs effectively.

Past studies have consistently shown that thoughtful material selection significantly impacts therapeutic outcomes. The Oxford Children's Center conducted a year-long study comparing spaces with traditional institutional materials to those with carefully selected sensory-friendly materials. Results showed that patients in the enhanced environments demonstrated better engagement in therapeutic activities and reported higher satisfaction levels. They achieved these improvements through a combination of durable base materials and replaceable sensory elements, allowing for both practical maintenance and therapeutic effectiveness.

Success in material implementation often requires a comprehensive approach that considers immediate needs and long-term sustainability. The Austin Therapeutic Complex exemplifies this through their phased implementation strategy, starting with essential elements and gradually expanding based on observed benefits and available resources. Their experience demonstrates that effective material selection can be achieved through careful planning and strategic implementation, regardless of initial budget constraints. They found that even modest material interventions, when thoughtfully planned and executed, can significantly improve the therapeutic environment while maintaining practical considerations for maintenance and durability.

Part 3: Room Specific Design

8. Bedroom Design

Sleep environment optimization begins with a comprehensive understanding of circadian rhythm principles and sensory needs. Research from the Stanford Sleep Institute demonstrates that carefully designed bedrooms can improve sleep quality. The Copenhagen Wellness Center pioneered an innovative "sleep sanctuary" approach, incorporating adjustable lighting systems that automatically dim in patterns mimicking natural sunset, along with sound-absorbing wall panels that reduce noise transmission. For facilities with limited budgets, similar effects can be achieved through strategic use of blackout curtains, white noise machines, and programmable LED bulbs. The Toronto Recovery Center implemented a cost-effective sleep optimization program using layered window treatments, creating varying levels of darkness for different times of day, while maintaining easy adjustment for individual preferences.

Personal space creation in therapeutic bedroom environments requires careful consideration of both physical and psychological boundaries. The Mayo Clinic's Environmental Psychology Department has shown that well-defined personal spaces can reduce anxiety and improve treatment outcomes. The Seattle Rehabilitation Facility demonstrated this principle by developing modular room divider systems that allow residents to easily modify their personal space. For budget-conscious facilities, similar results can be achieved using portable screens, curtain systems, or strategically placed furniture arrangements. The Portland Youth Center created effective personal zones using a combination of moveable furniture and fabric room dividers, allowing residents to adjust their space based on changing needs while maintaining a sense of security and ownership.

Storage solutions play a crucial role in maintaining therapeutic benefits while supporting daily functioning. The Amsterdam Design Institute's research indicates that visible clutter can increase stress levels and disrupt sleep patterns. Their findings led to the development of integrated storage systems that balance accessibility with visual calm. The Melbourne Treatment Center implemented these principles through a combination of built-in wardrobes with adjustable shelving and under-bed storage systems, accommodating different physical abilities and organizational needs. For facilities working with limited resources, effective storage can be achieved through the use of modular furniture systems, over-door organizers, and multi-functional pieces that maximize space efficiency while maintaining a calm environment.

Creating effective comfort zones within bedroom spaces requires attention to both physical and sensory comfort. The Berlin Therapeutic Center conducted a two-year study examining the impact of designated comfort areas on patient well-being. They found that rooms with clearly defined relaxation zones showed improved patient outcomes and higher satisfaction rates. The Vancouver Health Complex implemented these findings by creating multi-functional comfort corners using soft seating, adjustable lighting, and textured materials. For facilities operating on restricted budgets, similar effects can be achieved through the strategic placement of comfortable seating, soft textiles, and personal items that promote a sense of security and relaxation.

The incorporation of therapeutic principles in bedroom design must consider both immediate needs and long-term adaptability. The Chicago Mental Health Center developed an innovative approach using adaptable furniture systems that could be easily modified for different user needs. Their design included adjustable bed heights, moveable nightstands with various storage options, and flexible lighting solutions that could be customized for individual preferences. This approach can be scaled for different budgets through the use of furniture risers, clip-on reading lights, and modular storage units that allow for customization without permanent modifications.

Research from the University of Michigan's Environmental Design Lab demonstrates that successful bedroom design must address both sensory regulation and practical functionality. The Boston Recovery Center implemented these findings through a comprehensive design strategy that included sensory-sensitive material choices, adjustable ambient lighting, and modifiable storage solutions. They created environments that could be easily personalized while maintaining therapeutic benefits, using a combination of fixed elements for stability and moveable components for flexibility.

Past studies consistently show that thoughtful bedroom design significantly impacts therapeutic outcomes. The London Rehabilitation Institute conducted a comparative study of traditional institutional bedrooms versus therapeutically designed spaces. Results showed that patients in optimized environments demonstrated better sleep quality and reported higher levels of emotional well-being. They achieved these improvements through a combination of essential design elements and adaptable features, proving that effective therapeutic environments can be created across various budget levels.

Success in therapeutic bedroom design often comes from a balanced approach that considers both immediate comfort and long-term functionality. The Sydney Wellness Center exemplifies this through their tiered implementation strategy, focusing first on essential elements like lighting and sound control, then gradually adding enhanced features based on observed benefits and available resources. Their experience shows that effective therapeutic bedrooms can be created through careful planning and strategic implementation, regardless of initial budget constraints, always prioritizing the core elements that support sleep quality and personal well-being.

9. Bathroom Adaptation

Safety features in therapeutic bathroom environments require a comprehensive approach that balances protection with dignity. Research from the Healthcare Design Institute demonstrates that well-designed safety features can reduce bathroom accidents while maintaining a non-institutional appearance. The Stockholm Medical Center pioneered an innovative approach using integrated grab bars that double as towel rails, featuring warm-touch materials and aesthetic finishes that complement the overall design. For facilities with limited budgets, similar effects can be achieved through strategic placement of standard safety equipment enhanced with decorative elements. The Toronto Rehabilitation Center implemented a cost-effective safety program using textured non-slip flooring patterns that create visual interest while reducing fall risks, and installing LED strip lighting under vanities for nighttime visibility without harsh overhead glare.

Accessibility solutions must address diverse needs while promoting independence. The Mayo Clinic's Universal Design Department has shown that thoughtfully designed accessible bathrooms can increase user independence. The Vancouver Treatment Facility demonstrated this principle through their implementation of adjustable-height sinks with knee clearance, pull-out steps integrated into cabinetry, and easy-grip fixtures that accommodate various abilities. For budget-conscious facilities, effective accessibility can be achieved through modular solutions like removable mirror tilts, portable shower seats, and lever-handle adaptors for existing fixtures. The Portland Care Center created an adaptable bathroom system using mobile storage units and removable support rails, allowing for quick modifications based on changing user needs while maintaining structural integrity.

Sensory considerations play a vital role in creating comfortable and usable bathroom spaces. Research from the Sensory Design Institute shows that bathrooms with carefully controlled acoustics and lighting can reduce anxiety and promote better use of facilities. The Helsinki Wellness Center implemented these findings through a multi-layered approach to lighting that includes dimmable LED fixtures, natural light tubes, and motion-activated night lighting. They also incorporated sound-dampening materials and white noise features to maintain privacy and reduce echoing. For facilities working with limited resources, similar effects can be achieved through simple interventions like textured shower curtains that reduce noise, anti-glare films on mirrors, and timers for ventilation fans to manage sensory input.

Independence promotion requires thoughtful design that anticipates user needs while encouraging self-sufficiency. The Sydney Rehabilitation Institute conducted a year-long study examining how bathroom design elements impact user independence. Their findings led to the development of a "zones of use" concept, where toiletries, towels, and personal items are arranged in clearly defined areas based on typical usage patterns. The Chicago Medical Center adapted these principles using color-coded storage systems and illustrated guides for sequential tasks, helping users maintain independence in their daily routines. Budget-friendly implementations include using clear containers for organizing personal items, installing motion-sensor soap dispensers, and creating visual task sequences using waterproof cards.

The integration of therapeutic principles in bathroom design must address both physical and psychological comfort. The Amsterdam Care Facility developed an innovative approach using nature-inspired design elements that create a calming environment while maintaining practical functionality. Their design included moisture-resistant botanical wall coverings, marine-themed non-slip floor patterns, and nature sounds integrated into the ventilation system. For facilities with limited resources, similar effects can be achieved through waterproof nature photographs, ocean-colored tile accents, and portable sound machines.

Past studies demonstrate that successful bathroom adaptations significantly impact user confidence and independence. The Melbourne Wellness Center conducted a six-month comparison study between traditional and therapeutically adapted bathrooms. Results showed that users of adapted spaces demonstrated greater independence in daily routines and reported higher satisfaction levels. They achieved these improvements through a combination of essential safety features and customizable elements that could be adjusted for individual needs.

Engineering effective bathroom solutions often requires creative problem-solving to address multiple needs simultaneously. The Berlin Health Complex exemplifies this through their modular bathroom design system, which allows for easy modifications as user needs change. They implemented a track system for shower seats and grab bars that can be easily repositioned, along with adjustable mirrors and storage solutions that accommodate users of different heights and abilities. This approach can be scaled for different budgets through the use of removable adaptations and multi-purpose fixtures that serve both functional and therapeutic purposes.

Long-term success in bathroom adaptations comes from combining immediate safety needs with future adaptability. The Denver Rehabilitation Center demonstrates this through their phased implementation strategy, starting with essential safety features and gradually adding sensory and independence-promoting elements based on user feedback and available resources. Their experience shows that effective therapeutic bathrooms can be created through careful planning and strategic implementation, regardless of initial budget constraints, always prioritizing solutions that promote both safety and dignity while supporting independence.

10. Play Areas

Creating distinct stimulating and calming zones within play areas requires careful consideration of spatial flow and sensory management. Research from the Child Development Institute demonstrates that well-designed play zones can improve therapeutic outcomes. The Stockholm Children's Center pioneered an innovative "gradient approach" where play spaces transition smoothly from high-energy to calming areas through thoughtful use of colors, textures, and activity types. Their design includes active zones with climbing structures and movement-based activities, gradually transitioning to quiet corners with sensory walls and reading nooks. For facilities with limited budgets, similar effects can be achieved through strategic furniture arrangement, portable activity stations, and modular room dividers. The Toronto Youth Center implemented a cost-effective zoning system using different flooring materials and ceiling heights to naturally define activity areas while maintaining visual connection between spaces.

Safety considerations in therapeutic play areas must balance risk management with developmental benefits. The Mayo Clinic's Pediatric Research Division has shown that including controlled challenge elements in play spaces can improve motor skills and confidence. The Vancouver Children's Hospital demonstrated this principle through their innovative "safe challenge" system, incorporating adjustable climbing elements with impact-absorbing surfaces and graduated difficulty levels. For budget-conscious facilities, effective safety measures can include using modular foam climbing blocks, adjustable-height activity tables, and soft barrier systems that define spaces without restricting movement. The Portland Therapy Center created a safe but engaging environment using a combination of commercial and custom-made equipment, proving that effective play spaces can be created without premium-priced specialized equipment.

Equipment selection must address diverse therapeutic needs while maintaining engagement and adaptability. Research from the University of Michigan's Therapeutic Play Lab indicates that multi-functional equipment can increase user engagement. The Melbourne Children's Clinic implemented these findings through a system of convertible play structures that can be reconfigured for different therapeutic goals. Their equipment includes adjustable sensory panels, moveable climbing elements, and modular activity stations that can be modified based on individual needs. For facilities working with limited resources, similar versatility can be achieved through mobile equipment carts, reversible activity boards, and multi-purpose play materials that serve various therapeutic objectives.

Flexibility in design emerges as a crucial element for successful therapeutic play spaces. The Berlin Youth Center conducted a two-year study examining how adaptable play environments impact therapeutic outcomes. Their findings led to the development of a "zones of play" concept where spaces can be quickly reconfigured for different activities and group sizes. The Chicago Rehabilitation Center adapted these principles using mobile storage units, lightweight room dividers, and easily moveable furniture to create spaces that could transform throughout the day. Budget-friendly implementations include using wheeled furniture, hanging curtain track systems for quick space division, and stackable equipment that can be easily stored when not in use.

The integration of sensory elements in play area design requires careful attention to both stimulation and regulation needs. The Oslo Children's Hospital developed an innovative approach using interactive sensory walls that can be adjusted for different stimulation levels. Their design included textured climbing surfaces, light-up activity panels, and sound-dampening zones for sensory breaks. For facilities with limited resources, similar effects can be achieved through DIY sensory boards, portable light tables, and simple switch-activated cause-and-effect toys.

Past studies demonstrate that successful play areas significantly impact therapeutic engagement and outcomes. The Sydney Children's Center conducted a comparative study between traditional playrooms and therapeutically designed spaces. Results showed that children in optimized environments demonstrated better engagement in therapeutic activities and showed improved social interaction. They achieved these improvements through a combination of essential play elements and adaptable features that could be modified for different therapeutic goals.

Long-term success in play area design often comes from a comprehensive approach that considers both immediate needs and future adaptability. The Austin Therapeutic Center exemplifies this through their phased implementation strategy, starting with essential play elements and gradually adding enhanced features based on observed benefits and available resources. Their experience shows that effective therapeutic play spaces can be created through careful planning and strategic implementation, regardless of initial budget constraints.

Integration of technology in play areas requires thoughtful consideration of therapeutic benefits and practical limitations. The Helsinki Children's Hospital pioneered a hybrid approach combining traditional play equipment with interactive technology elements. They created zones where digital and physical play could complement each other, using projection systems for interactive floor games and simple touch-activated sound panels. For facilities with limited technology budgets, similar engagement can be achieved through basic motion sensors, timer systems for activities, and simple cause-and-effect devices that enhance traditional play equipment.

11. Study Spaces

Focus-enhancing design in study spaces requires a careful balance of stimulation and calm. Research from the Educational Environment Institute demonstrates that well-designed study areas can improve concentration. The Stockholm Learning Center pioneered an innovative "focus pod" system, incorporating adjustable privacy screens, sound-absorbing materials, and personalized lighting controls. For facilities with limited budgets, similar effects can be achieved through the strategic use of bookcases as room dividers, portable desk partitions, and task lighting. The Toronto Educational Center implemented a cost-effective focus enhancement program using modular study carrels with adjustable walls and built-in lighting, proving that effective study environments can be created without extensive renovation.

Organizational systems play a crucial role in supporting cognitive function and reducing stress in study environments. The Harvard Learning Lab has shown that intuitive organization systems can reduce task-switching time and decrease study-related anxiety. The Vancouver Academic Center demonstrated this principle through their implementation of color-coded storage zones, clear labeling systems, and dedicated spaces for different study materials. For budget-conscious facilities, effective organization can be achieved through the use of transparent containers, magnetic wall systems, and modular desk organizers that can be customized for different subjects and learning styles. The Portland Study Center created an adaptable organization system using mobile storage units and wall-mounted planning boards, allowing students to modify their space based on changing academic needs.

Lighting for learning requires sophisticated understanding of how different light qualities affect cognitive performance. Research from the University of Michigan's Environmental Psychology Department indicates that proper lighting can improve reading comprehension and reduce eye strain. The Melbourne Educational Facility implemented these findings through a multi-layered lighting approach that includes adjustable task lighting, ambient illumination with variable color temperatures, and natural light optimization. For facilities working with limited resources, effective lighting can be achieved through the strategic placement of desk lamps with different color temperature options, window treatments that control glare, and reflective surfaces that maximize natural light distribution.

Minimizing distractions involves both physical design elements and psychological considerations. The Oslo Learning Institute conducted a year-long study examining how different environmental factors impact study concentration. Their findings led to the development of a "zone of concentration" concept where visual, auditory, and movement distractions are systematically reduced through design. The Chicago Academic Center adapted these principles using acoustic panels, directional lighting, and strategic furniture placement to create focused study environments. Budget-friendly implementations include using portable sound barriers, desk-mounted privacy screens, and simple white noise machines to mask disruptive sounds.

The integration of therapeutic principles in study space design must address both cognitive and emotional needs. The Amsterdam Educational Center developed an innovative approach using biophilic design elements that promote calm focus while maintaining academic functionality. Their design included natural materials, plants selected for low maintenance, and nature-inspired color schemes proven to reduce stress. For facilities with limited resources, similar effects can be achieved through the use of nature photographs, small indoor plants, and natural textures in furniture and accessories.

Past studies demonstrate that thoughtfully designed study spaces significantly impact academic performance and well-being. The Berlin Learning Center conducted a six-month comparison study between traditional and therapeutically designed study areas. Results showed that students in optimized environments demonstrated better task completion rates and reported lower stress levels. They achieved these improvements through a combination of essential design elements and adaptable features that could be modified for different learning styles and needs.

Success in study space design often requires a comprehensive approach that considers both immediate functionality and long-term adaptability. The Sydney Academic Institute exemplifies this through their phased implementation strategy, starting with essential elements like proper lighting and basic organization systems, then gradually adding enhanced features based on observed benefits and available resources. Their experience shows that effective therapeutic study spaces can be created through careful planning and strategic implementation, regardless of initial budget constraints.

The integration of technology in study spaces must balance digital tools with traditional learning methods. The Munich Educational Center pioneered a hybrid approach combining quiet study areas with technology-enabled zones. They created spaces where students could easily transition between digital and analog work while maintaining focus and organization. For facilities with limited technology budgets, similar functionality can be achieved through simple charging stations, designated device-free zones, and basic cable management systems that keep technology organized but not intrusive.

Part 4 Specialized Spaces

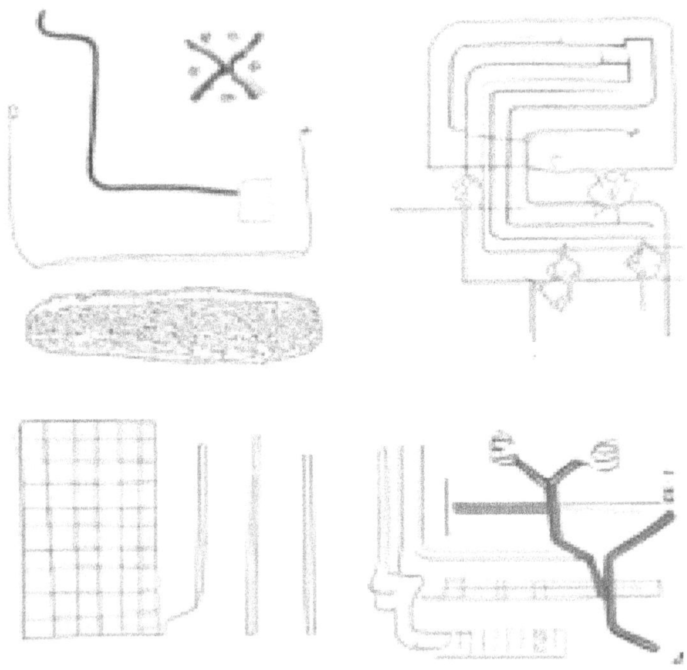

12. Sensory Rooms

Essential components in sensory rooms must be carefully selected to provide comprehensive sensory experiences while maintaining therapeutic effectiveness. Research from the Sensory Integration Institute demonstrates that well-designed sensory rooms can improve self-regulation. The Stockholm Therapy Center pioneered an innovative "sensory mapping" approach, incorporating distinct zones for vestibular, proprioceptive, tactile, visual, and auditory stimulation. For facilities with limited budgets, essential elements can include adjustable lighting systems using LED strips and projectors, textured wall panels created from readily available materials, and simple sound systems with nature sounds. The Toronto Children's Hospital implemented a cost-effective sensory program using a combination of DIY solutions and carefully selected commercial equipment, proving that effective sensory environments can be created without premium-priced specialized equipment.

Equipment selection must balance therapeutic benefits with practical considerations of durability and maintenance. The Mayo Clinic's Sensory Research Division has shown that multi-functional equipment can increase user engagement while reducing overall costs. The Vancouver Treatment Center demonstrated this principle through their implementation of convertible sensory equipment that serves multiple therapeutic purposes. Their design includes adjustable swing systems that can be reconfigured for different activities, modular climbing elements that double as proprioceptive input tools, and interactive light panels that provide both visual and tactile stimulation. For budget-conscious facilities, effective equipment solutions can include items like lycra tunnels that provide both movement and pressure input, weighted blankets with washable covers, and portable bubble tubes with color-changing capabilities.

Multi-purpose design emerges as a crucial element for maximizing space utility and therapeutic benefits. The Berlin Sensory Institute conducted a two-year study examining how adaptable sensory environments impact therapeutic outcomes. Their findings led to the development of a "flexible zones" concept where spaces can be quickly reconfigured for different sensory needs and group sizes. The Chicago Rehabilitation Center adapted these principles using mobile equipment stations, ceiling-mounted track systems for hanging equipment, and modular floor mats that can be arranged in various configurations. Budget-friendly implementations include using room dividers on wheels, inflatable sensory equipment that can be easily stored, and multi-purpose sensory bins that can be modified for different activities.

Budget considerations require creative solutions that maintain therapeutic effectiveness while managing costs. The Melbourne Children's

Center developed an innovative approach to phased implementation, starting with essential elements and gradually adding more sophisticated equipment as resources became available. Their strategy included creating a foundation of basic sensory equipment like crash pads, swings, and light projectors, then expanding with more specialized items based on observed needs. For facilities working with limited resources, similar results can be achieved through DIY solutions like creating tactile walls using different textured materials, using fabric panels for visual division, and incorporating natural materials for sensory exploration.

The integration of technology in sensory rooms must be carefully balanced with non-digital sensory experiences. The Oslo Therapy Center pioneered a hybrid approach combining traditional sensory equipment with interactive technology. Their design includes projection systems that respond to movement, sound-responsive lighting, and simple touch-activated sensory panels. For facilities with limited technology budgets, similar engagement can be achieved through basic motion sensors, timer systems for activities, and simple cause-and-effect devices that enhance traditional sensory equipment.

Past studies demonstrate that successful sensory rooms significantly impact therapeutic outcomes. The Sydney Children's Hospital conducted a comparative study between traditional therapy spaces and properly equipped sensory rooms. Results showed that children in optimized sensory environments demonstrated better self-regulation skills and showed improved engagement in therapeutic activities. They achieved these improvements through a combination of essential sensory elements and adaptable features that could be modified for different therapeutic goals.

Long-term success in sensory room design often comes from a comprehensive approach that considers both immediate needs and future adaptability. The Austin Therapeutic Center exemplifies this through their tiered implementation strategy, starting with essential sensory elements and gradually adding enhanced features based on observed benefits and available resources. Their experience shows that effective sensory rooms can be created through careful planning and strategic implementation, regardless of initial budget constraints.

Maintenance and safety considerations must be integrated into every aspect of sensory room design. The Helsinki Children's Center developed a systematic approach to equipment maintenance and cleaning protocols while maintaining therapeutic effectiveness. Their design included easily cleanable surfaces, removable covers for soft equipment, and modular components that could be quickly inspected and replaced when needed. For facilities with limited maintenance budgets, similar standards can be maintained through careful selection of durable materials, implementation of regular cleaning schedules, and use of protective covers for sensitive equipment.

13. Therapy Spaces at Home

Physical therapy areas in home environments require careful consideration of both space utilization and therapeutic effectiveness. Research from the Home Healthcare Institute demonstrates that well-designed home therapy spaces can improve treatment adherence. The Stockholm Home Care Program pioneered an innovative "zone transformation" approach, where living spaces can quickly convert to therapy areas using mobile equipment and adaptable furniture. For homes with limited space, effective solutions include using folding exercise mats, door-mounted pulleys, and collapsible parallel bars. The Toronto Rehabilitation Network implemented a cost-effective home therapy program using multi-purpose furniture pieces that serve both daily living and therapeutic needs, such as adjustable height tables that work for both dining and therapy exercises.

Occupational therapy spaces in the home environment must balance therapeutic requirements with practical living needs. The Mayo Clinic's Home Adaptation Study has shown that thoughtfully designed home therapy spaces can increase independence in daily activities. The Vancouver Home Care Center demonstrated this principle through their implementation of modular activity stations that can be easily modified for different therapy goals. Their design includes adjustable-height counters for kitchen activities, removable adaptive equipment for bathroom tasks, and convertible workstations for fine motor activities. For families working with limited budgets, effective solutions can include using tension rods for temporary grab bars, removable cabinet hardware for grip practice, and adjustable lighting for visual processing activities.

Speech therapy considerations require attention to both acoustic properties and communication support needs. Research from the Communication Disorders Institute indicates that properly designed home therapy spaces can improve session effectiveness. The Melbourne Family Center developed an innovative approach using portable acoustic panels, designated therapy corners with minimal visual distractions, and easily accessible communication tools. For homes with limited resources, similar effects can be achieved through strategic furniture placement to create quiet zones, use of carpet remnants for sound absorption, and creation of visual communication boards using household materials.

Adaptable furniture plays a crucial role in creating successful home therapy environments. The Berlin Home Health Study conducted a year-long examination of how furniture adaptability impacts therapy outcomes. Their findings led to the development of a "flexible furniture matrix" where standard household items could be modified for therapeutic use. The Chicago Home Care Program adapted these principles using adjustable table heights, modifiable seating options, and convertible storage solutions that support various therapy activities. Budget-friendly implementations include using furniture risers, cushion modifications, and DIY adaptive equipment holders.

The integration of therapeutic equipment with home décor requires creative solutions that maintain both functionality and aesthetics. The Amsterdam Home Design Center pioneered an approach combining therapeutic necessities with interior design principles. Their solutions included decorative wall-mounted balance bars, attractive storage solutions for therapy equipment, and dual-purpose furniture that blends with home décor. For families with limited resources, similar results can be achieved through creative camouflaging of equipment, use of decorative screens for privacy, and integration of therapy tools into existing furniture arrangements.

Past studies demonstrate that well-designed home therapy spaces significantly impact treatment success. The Sydney Home Therapy Program conducted a six-month comparison study between traditional home setups and therapeutically optimized spaces. Results showed that patients in adapted environments demonstrated better therapy adherence and reported higher satisfaction with home-based treatment. They achieved these improvements through a combination of essential adaptations and flexible solutions that could be modified as therapy needs changed.

Long-term success in home therapy spaces often requires a comprehensive approach that considers both immediate needs and future adaptability. The Austin Family Support Center exemplifies this through their phased implementation strategy, starting with essential modifications and gradually adding enhanced features based on therapeutic progress and available resources. Their experience shows that effective home therapy spaces can be created through careful planning and strategic implementation, regardless of initial budget constraints.

Storage and organization solutions become particularly crucial in home therapy environments. The Oslo Home Care Institute developed a systematic approach to equipment storage and accessibility while maintaining home functionality. Their design included vertical storage solutions, multi-purpose containers, and clearly labeled organization systems that both family members and therapists could easily navigate. For homes with limited storage space, similar organization can be achieved through under-bed storage solutions, over-door organizers, and mobile therapy carts that can be moved between rooms as needed.

Success in home therapy space design often depends on the ability to quickly transition between therapy and daily living uses. The Helsinki Family Center demonstrates this through their innovative use of murphy-style therapy equipment storage, sliding room dividers, and modular furniture systems that support both therapeutic and everyday activities. Their approach shows that with thoughtful planning, homes can effectively accommodate therapy needs without sacrificing comfort or functionality in daily living spaces.

14. Outdoor Spaces

Sensory gardens represent a crucial element in therapeutic outdoor design, combining natural elements with intentional sensory experiences. Research from the Therapeutic Landscape Institute demonstrates that well-designed sensory gardens can reduce stress levels. The Stockholm Wellness Center pioneered an innovative "sensory pathway" approach, creating distinct zones for different sensory experiences using varied plant textures, aromatic herbs, and interactive water features. For facilities with limited budgets, effective sensory gardens can be created using raised planter boxes with different textured plants, wind chimes for auditory stimulation, and simple water features made from recycled materials. The Toronto Healing Center implemented a cost-effective sensory garden using native plants, recycled materials for pathways, and locally sourced natural elements, proving that therapeutic outdoor spaces can be created without extensive landscaping costs.

Play equipment in therapeutic outdoor spaces must balance challenge and safety while supporting developmental goals. The Mayo Clinic's Outdoor Therapy Research shows that natural play elements can improve motor skills development compared to traditional playground equipment. The Vancouver Children's Hospital demonstrated this through their implementation of "natural playground" concepts, incorporating climbing logs, boulder formations, and balance beams made from natural materials. For organizations working with limited resources, similar benefits can be achieved through strategic use of fallen logs, natural climbing rocks, and sand play areas. The Portland Therapy Center created an effective outdoor play space using a combination of natural elements and simple adaptable equipment, showcasing how therapeutic benefits can be achieved through thoughtful design rather than expensive specialized equipment.

Safety measures in outdoor therapeutic spaces require comprehensive planning while maintaining natural appeal. Research from the Environmental Design Institute indicates that well-integrated safety features can reduce accidents without compromising therapeutic benefits. The Melbourne Rehabilitation Center developed an innovative approach using different ground surfaces to naturally define activity zones, incorporating impact-absorbing materials beneath climbing areas, and creating clear sightlines for supervision. Budget-conscious facilities can implement safety measures through the use of rubber mulch in fall zones, clearly marked pathway edges with natural materials, and strategic placement of seating for supervision.

Nature integration serves as the foundation for therapeutic outdoor spaces, requiring careful consideration of both aesthetic and functional elements. The Berlin Garden Therapy Institute conducted a two-year study examining how different natural elements impact therapeutic outcomes. Their findings led to the development of an "ecological therapy" approach where native plants, natural materials, and wildlife-friendly features create a holistic healing environment. The Chicago Wellness Center adapted these principles using butterfly gardens, sensory-rich native plants, and water features that attract local wildlife. Cost-effective implementations include creating wildlife habitats using native plants, installing bird feeders and houses, and developing rain gardens that serve both therapeutic and ecological functions.

The integration of accessibility features in natural settings requires creative solutions that maintain the outdoor experience. The Oslo Therapeutic Gardens pioneered an approach combining accessible pathways with immersive natural experiences. Their design includes gently graded trails, raised garden beds at various heights, and tactile navigation aids integrated into natural elements. For facilities with limited resources, similar accessibility can be achieved through stabilized gravel paths, modular raised beds, and strategic placement of rest areas.

Past studies demonstrate that well-designed outdoor therapeutic spaces significantly impact treatment outcomes. The Sydney Children's Hospital conducted a comparative study between traditional therapy spaces and nature-integrated environments. Results showed that patients in natural settings demonstrated better engagement in therapy activities and showed improved emotional regulation. They achieved these improvements through a combination of essential natural elements and adaptable features that could be modified for different therapeutic goals.

Success in outdoor therapeutic design often comes from a comprehensive approach that considers seasonal changes and maintenance requirements. The Austin Healing Center exemplifies this through their four-season design strategy, ensuring therapeutic benefits throughout the year using evergreen plants, covered activity areas, and weather-resistant equipment. Their experience shows that effective outdoor therapy spaces can maintain functionality year-round through careful planning and strategic plant selection.

Long-term maintenance considerations must be integrated into the initial design process. The Helsinki Wellness Complex developed a sustainable maintenance approach that balances therapeutic effectiveness with practical upkeep requirements. Their design included drought-resistant plants, low-maintenance natural play elements, and easily replaceable sensory components. For facilities with limited maintenance budgets, similar sustainability can be achieved through careful plant selection, use of durable natural materials, and implementation of volunteer maintenance programs.

Part 5: Practical Implementation

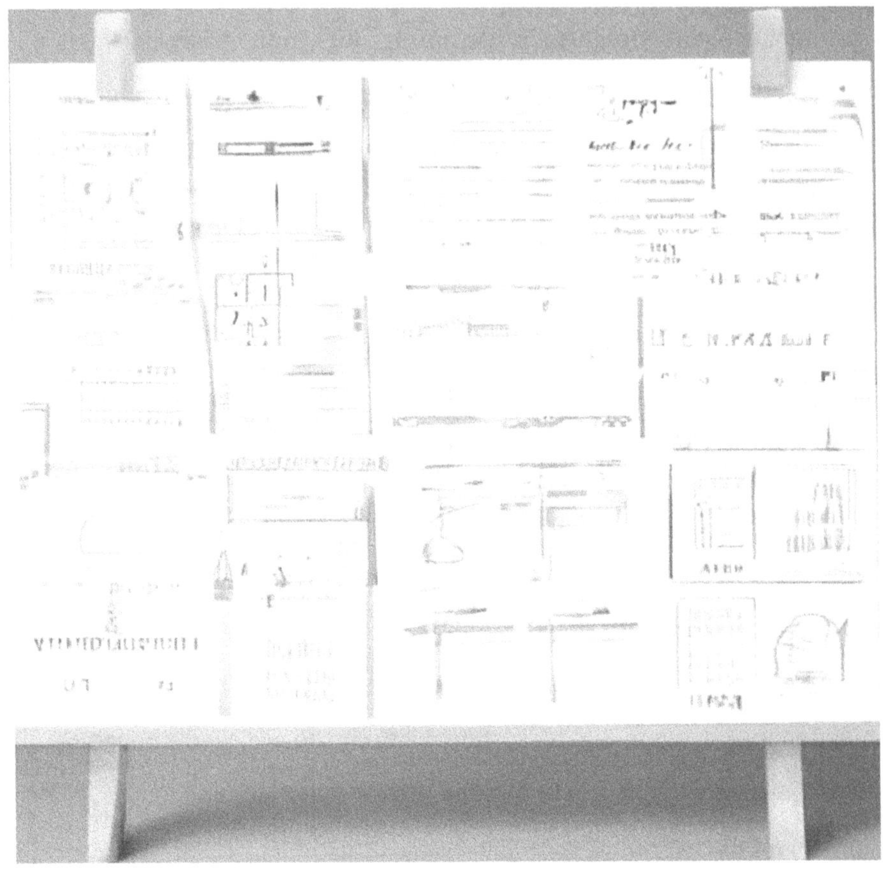

15. Budget-Friendly Solutions

DIY adaptations represent a crucial strategy for creating effective therapeutic spaces on limited budgets. Research from the Adaptive Design Institute demonstrates that well-executed DIY modifications can achieve the benefits of commercial solutions at a fraction of the cost. The Stockholm Community Center pioneered an innovative "maker space" approach, creating custom therapeutic equipment using readily available materials. Their solutions included sensory walls made from household items, balance equipment created from PVC pipes, and communication boards using digital printing services. The Toronto Rehabilitation Network implemented a successful DIY program where therapists and maintenance staff collaborated to create custom solutions, such as adjustable therapy tables made from modified dining tables and sensory integration equipment built from basic hardware store materials.

Phased implementation strategy emerges as a key approach for managing costs while maintaining therapeutic effectiveness. The Mayo Clinic's Resource Management Study shows that carefully planned phasing can reduce initial costs while ensuring essential therapeutic elements are prioritized. The Vancouver Treatment Center demonstrated this principle through their "essential first" implementation plan, starting with critical adaptations and gradually adding enhanced features as funding became available. Their approach included beginning with basic safety modifications and core therapeutic equipment, then systematically adding sensory elements and specialized features over time. For facilities with very limited resources, successful phasing can start with mobile equipment that serves multiple purposes, temporary adaptations that can be easily upgraded, and modular solutions that allow for gradual expansion.

Resource maximization requires creative thinking and strategic planning to optimize available materials and space. The Berlin Healthcare Institute conducted a year-long study examining how resource optimization impacts therapeutic outcomes. Their findings led to the development of a "multi-use matrix" where spaces and equipment serve multiple therapeutic purposes throughout the day. The Chicago Community Center adapted these principles by creating convertible therapy spaces using mobile partition systems, multi-purpose furniture, and adaptable storage solutions. Budget-friendly implementations include using tension rods for temporary therapy equipment mounting, repurposing everyday items for therapeutic activities, and creating modular equipment that can be reconfigured for different uses.

Cost-effective materials selection plays a vital role in creating sustainable therapeutic environments. Research from the Environmental Design Lab indicates that carefully chosen alternative materials can provide comparable therapeutic benefits while reducing costs. The

Melbourne Therapy Center developed an innovative approach using industrial materials repurposed for therapeutic use, such as commercial floor tiles for sensory pathways and warehouse shelving systems modified for therapy equipment storage. For organizations working with minimal budgets, effective solutions include using vinyl flooring remnants for movement zones, recycled materials for sensory equipment, and bulk-purchased basic materials that can be adapted for multiple purposes.

The integration of community resources can significantly extend limited budgets. The Oslo Community Health Center pioneered a collaborative approach, partnering with local businesses and craftspeople to create custom therapeutic solutions at reduced costs. Their program included working with carpentry students for custom furniture, partnering with art programs for sensory wall murals, and engaging community volunteers for maintenance tasks. This model demonstrates how networking and creative partnerships can maximize limited resources while maintaining therapeutic quality.

Past studies consistently show that budget-conscious design can achieve significant therapeutic benefits. The Sydney Children's Hospital conducted a comparative study between high-end commercial solutions and thoughtfully implemented budget-friendly alternatives. Results showed that well-planned budget spaces achieved the therapeutic outcomes at less cost. They accomplished this through careful material selection, strategic phasing of implementations, and creative adaptation of existing resources.

Success in budget-friendly implementation often requires a comprehensive understanding of both immediate needs and long-term sustainability. The Austin Therapeutic Center exemplifies this through their "sustainable growth" model, starting with essential elements and gradually expanding based on documented outcomes and available resources. Their experience shows that effective therapeutic environments can be created through careful planning and creative resource utilization, regardless of initial budget constraints.

Long-term cost management must be integrated into initial design decisions. The Helsinki Rehabilitation Institute developed a systematic approach to budget-friendly design that considers both immediate costs and long-term maintenance requirements. Their strategy included selecting durable materials that require minimal maintenance, implementing easily repairable solutions, and creating detailed maintenance protocols that prevent costly repairs. For facilities with limited maintenance budgets, similar sustainability can be achieved through careful material selection, preventive maintenance schedules, and staff training in basic repairs and adaptations.

16. Safety and Accessibility

Building codes compliance in therapeutic environments requires a comprehensive understanding of both regulatory requirements and therapeutic needs. Research from the Universal Design Institute demonstrates that well-integrated building code compliance can enhance therapeutic outcomes while ensuring safety. The Stockholm Rehabilitation Center pioneered an innovative "integrated compliance" approach, where therapeutic features are seamlessly incorporated into required safety elements. For facilities with limited budgets, effective compliance can be achieved through careful space planning that maximizes the therapeutic value of required safety features, such as using handrails as balance training elements or incorporating required turning radiuses into activity spaces. The Toronto Medical Center implemented a cost-effective compliance program by creating multi-functional spaces that meet code requirements while serving therapeutic purposes, proving that safety and therapeutic value can coexist within budget constraints.

ADA guidelines implementation must balance accessibility requirements with therapeutic functionality. The Mayo Clinic's Access Design Study shows that thoughtfully implemented ADA features can improve therapeutic outcomes by enabling greater independence. The Vancouver Treatment Facility demonstrated this through their implementation of universal design principles that exceed minimum ADA requirements while enhancing therapeutic opportunities. Their design includes adjustable-height surfaces that accommodate both wheelchair users and standing therapy, accessible storage solutions that promote independence, and clear wayfinding systems that support cognitive accessibility. For organizations working with limited resources, effective accessibility can be achieved through modular ramp systems, removable accessibility aids, and strategic furniture placement that maintains clear paths while maximizing therapeutic space.

Risk assessment processes require systematic evaluation of both obvious and subtle safety concerns. The Berlin Safety Institute conducted a two-year study examining how comprehensive risk assessment impacts facility safety outcomes. Their findings led to the development of a "therapeutic risk matrix" where potential hazards are evaluated against therapeutic benefits to find optimal solutions. The Chicago Rehabilitation Center adapted these principles using a tiered risk assessment system that prioritizes critical safety needs while maintaining therapeutic effectiveness. Cost-effective implementations include creating detailed safety protocols, implementing regular safety audits, and developing staff training programs that address both safety requirements and therapeutic goals.

Emergency considerations must address both standard safety requirements and the specific needs of therapeutic environments. Research from the Healthcare Safety Network indicates that well-designed emergency systems can reduce response times in therapeutic settings. The Melbourne Treatment Center developed an innovative approach to emergency planning that integrates therapeutic considerations with safety requirements. Their system includes clear evacuation routes that accommodate mobility devices, emergency equipment storage that doesn't interfere with therapeutic activities, and communication systems adapted for various abilities. For facilities with limited resources, effective emergency planning can include creating simple, clear evacuation maps, implementing regular emergency drills, and developing backup plans for therapeutic equipment during emergencies.

Past studies demonstrate that comprehensive safety and accessibility planning significantly impacts both compliance and therapeutic outcomes. The Sydney Wellness Center conducted a comparative study between minimum compliance approaches and therapeutically integrated safety systems. Results showed that integrated approaches improved both safety outcomes and therapeutic engagement. They achieved these improvements through careful planning that considered both regulatory requirements and therapeutic needs from the initial design phase.

Long-term success in safety and accessibility often requires a proactive approach to maintenance and updates. The Austin Therapeutic Complex exemplifies this through their "continuous compliance" strategy, regularly reviewing and updating safety features to meet both changing regulations and evolving therapeutic needs. Their experience shows that effective safety and accessibility can be maintained through systematic monitoring and timely updates, regardless of budget constraints.

Integration of new safety technologies must balance innovation with practicality. The Oslo Health Center pioneered an approach combining traditional safety features with modern monitoring systems. Their design includes smart sensors for fall prevention, automated emergency response systems, and digital tracking of safety compliance. For facilities with limited technology budgets, similar safety enhancement can be achieved through simple motion sensors, basic emergency alert systems, and regular safety audits using digital checklists.

Success in safety and accessibility implementation often depends on staff training and engagement. The Helsinki Rehabilitation Institute developed a comprehensive training program that ensures all staff understand both safety requirements and therapeutic implications. Their approach includes regular safety workshops, hands-on accessibility training, and continuous feedback systems for identifying potential safety concerns. This model demonstrates how effective safety and accessibility programs can be maintained through staff education and engagement, even with limited resources.

17. Technology and Integration

Smart home features in therapeutic environments require careful consideration of both functionality and user accessibility. Research from the Assistive Technology Institute demonstrates that well-implemented smart home systems can increase independence. The Stockholm Rehabilitation Center pioneered an innovative "layered technology" approach, where smart features are introduced gradually based on user comfort and therapeutic needs. For facilities with limited budgets, effective smart home implementation can begin with basic voice-controlled lighting, programmable thermostats, and simple automated routines. The Toronto Care Center implemented a cost-effective smart home program using affordable hub systems and modular components that could be expanded over time, proving that effective technology integration can be achieved without premium automation systems.

Assistive technologies must balance technological sophistication with practical usability. The Mayo Clinic's Adaptive Technology Study shows that thoughtfully selected assistive devices can improve daily task completion. The Vancouver Treatment Facility demonstrated this through their implementation of scalable assistive technology solutions, ranging from basic switch adaptations to advanced eye-tracking systems. Their approach includes adjustable mounting systems for tablets and communication devices, universal charging stations, and adaptable control interfaces. For organizations working with limited resources, effective solutions can include using standard tablets with specialized apps, creating custom switch interfaces from affordable components, and implementing DIY mounting solutions for existing devices.

Monitoring systems require careful integration of privacy considerations with safety needs. The Berlin Healthcare Institute conducted a comprehensive study examining how different monitoring approaches impact both safety and user comfort. Their findings led to the development of a "privacy-first monitoring" framework where technology is implemented with clear user consent and control. The Chicago Rehabilitation Center adapted these principles using a combination of passive sensors, user-activated systems, and customizable privacy settings. Budget-friendly implementations include using motion sensors for basic activity monitoring, simple alert systems for emergency response, and scheduled virtual check-ins using standard communication devices.

Educational tech spaces must support various learning styles while maintaining therapeutic goals. Research from the Educational Technology Lab indicates that well-designed tech learning environments can improve skill acquisition. The Melbourne Learning Center developed an innovative approach combining traditional therapeutic tools with digital learning platforms. Their design includes adjustable workstations for different devices, integrated cable management systems, and flexible seating arrangements that support both individual and group technology use. For facilities with limited technology budgets, effective solutions include creating mobile tech stations, implementing shared device programs, and using open-source educational software.

Past studies demonstrate that successful technology integration significantly impacts therapeutic outcomes. The Sydney Therapy Center conducted a comparative study between traditional approaches and technology-enhanced therapeutic environments. Results showed that thoughtfully integrated technology improved engagement and treatment adherence. They achieved these improvements through a combination of essential technology tools and adaptable systems that could be modified for different user needs.

Long-term success in technology integration often requires a comprehensive approach to maintenance and updates. The Austin Treatment Complex exemplifies this through their "sustainable technology" strategy, focusing on reliable, easily maintainable systems rather than cutting-edge solutions. Their experience shows that effective technology integration can be achieved through careful planning and strategic implementation, regardless of initial budget constraints.

The integration of remote therapy capabilities has become increasingly important. The Oslo Health Center pioneered a hybrid approach combining in-person and remote therapy technologies. Their system includes dedicated video conferencing spaces, remote monitoring capabilities, and secure data sharing platforms. For facilities with limited resources, similar remote therapy support can be achieved through basic video conferencing setups, secure messaging systems, and simple progress tracking tools.

Success in technology implementation often depends on staff training and user support. The Helsinki Rehabilitation Institute developed a comprehensive technology training program that ensures both staff and users can effectively utilize available systems. Their approach includes regular technology workshops, step-by-step user guides, and ongoing technical support resources. This model demonstrates how effective technology integration can be maintained through education and support, even with limited resources.

Ensuring technology accessibility for diverse user needs requires careful consideration of interface design and physical access. The Amsterdam Care Center implemented an innovative universal design approach to their technology systems, ensuring that all devices and interfaces could be used by individuals with varying abilities. Their solutions include adjustable mounting systems, alternative input devices, and customizable user interfaces that can be modified based on individual needs and preferences.

Part 6: Special Considerations

18. Mutli-Child Spaces

Designing spaces for multiple children presents unique challenges that require thoughtful consideration of both individual needs and group dynamics. The key lies in creating environments that support independence while fostering healthy sibling relationships and maximizing available space for diverse activities.

When designing shared bedrooms, the fundamental principle is to establish clearly defined territories while maintaining a cohesive overall design. Consider implementing room dividers that serve multiple purposes - for instance, a double-sided bookshelf that acts as both a space separator and storage solution. In a recent project for 8- and 10-year-old siblings, a floor-to-ceiling rope-and-wood screen created semi-private areas while maintaining an open feel.

For budget-conscious families, simple solutions like using different wall colors or patterns on each side of the room can effectively delineate personal spaces. Curtain tracks mounted on the ceiling provide an affordable, flexible option for privacy, allowing children to open or close their spaces as needed. These solutions work particularly well for families in rental properties where permanent modifications aren't possible.

Even in shared environments, it's crucial to carve out personal territories that reflect each child's personality and preferences. Consider implementing "zones" within the shared space - study areas, reading nooks, and play spaces that can be personalized while maintaining visual harmony. A successful approach observed in therapeutic settings involves creating "micro-rooms" using corner spaces and portable screens, allowing children to retreat when they need alone time. A family with three children in a modest-sized room successfully implemented a triple-bunk system with built-in desks underneath, incorporating different color schemes and lighting options for each child. The design included removable desk panels that could transform into art easels, maximizing functionality in limited space.

Understanding the developmental stages and relationships between siblings is crucial for successful space design. For instance, children with significant age gaps may require different sleep schedules and study needs. Installation of adjustable task lighting and sound-dampening solutions becomes essential in these scenarios. Therapeutic principles suggest incorporating "peace corners" or shared calm-down spaces that siblings can use together or individually during conflicts. A notable example comes from a family with twins and an older sibling, where the room design included a central communal area for shared activities, flanked by individual "pods" for personal space. The design incorporated acoustic panels decorated with personalized artwork, serving both functional and aesthetic purposes.

Future-proofing shared spaces requires incorporating adaptable elements that can evolve with children's changing needs. Modular furniture systems, adjustable storage solutions, and mobile organization units allow for easy reconfiguration as children grow. Consider implementing furniture that serves multiple purposes - such as storage ottomans that function as seating, or desk systems that can be adjusted in height and configuration. A remarkable transformation involved a shared room for three sisters (ages 4, 7, and 10) using a modular wall system with interchangeable panels. The panels included whiteboard surfaces, cork boards, and magnetic sections, allowing each child to customize their space while maintaining the ability to modify the layout as needs changed.

When executing multi-child space designs, consider these practical recommendations:

Install adjustable lighting systems with individual controls for each child's area, allowing for personalized illumination without disturbing siblings. Utilize vertical space with wall-mounted storage solutions and lofted beds when appropriate, maximizing floor space for activities. Incorporate sound-absorbing materials through decorative elements like fabric wall hangings or acoustic panels designed as art pieces.

For varying budgets, solutions can range from DIY options like painted storage crates serving as room dividers to professional custom-built furniture systems. The key is maintaining functionality while addressing each child's need for personal space and expression.

From a therapeutic standpoint, multi-child spaces should promote both independence and healthy interaction. Include elements that encourage cooperation, such as shared activity tables with individual storage sections, while maintaining clear boundaries for personal possessions. Consider incorporating elements that support emotional regulation, such as quiet corners with comfort items accessible to all children.

The success of multi-child spaces often depends on involving children in the design process, allowing them to voice their preferences while teaching compromise and respect for siblings' needs. This collaborative approach not only results in more functional spaces but also helps develop important social skills and family bonds.

19. Transition Spaces

Transition spaces serve as crucial connecting points within therapeutic environments, acting as bridges between different activities and emotional states. These areas require thoughtful design to support smooth transitions, reduce anxiety, and promote independence while accommodating various sensory needs and organizational requirements.

Entry and exit points represent critical transition moments that can set the tone for the entire experience. These spaces should provide clear visual and physical cues that help individuals prepare for environmental changes. past Study: A pediatric therapy center in Seattle implemented a graduated entry system where the foyer transitioned from bright to softer lighting over a 15-foot span, allowing clients to adjust gradually while removing outerwear and storing belongings.

Consider incorporating decompression zones near entrances, featuring comfortable seating and calming elements like water features or nature-inspired artwork. For budget-conscious facilities, simple solutions such as painted pathway markers on the floor or wall-mounted coat hooks at varying heights can effectively organize the space. One particularly successful implementation involved using color-coded zones in the entry area, with each color corresponding to different activities or destinations within the facility.

Transitions between different functional spaces require careful consideration to maintain flow while providing necessary breaks between activities. Wide, well-lit corridors with built-in pause points allow individuals to prepare for environmental changes. A school therapy wing created "transition nooks" every 20 feet along hallways, featuring small benches and visual schedules, providing students with designated spots to gather themselves between activities.

For facilities with limited space, wall-mounted flip-down seats or standing pause points marked with floor decals offer cost-effective solutions. Consider implementing graduated changes in flooring materials or wall colors to signal transitions, using patterns that guide movement without causing sensory overload. One innovative approach involved using LED strip lighting along baseboards to create subtle directional cues, with different colors indicating different destination types.

Effective visual scheduling systems are essential for reducing transition-related anxiety and promoting independence. These systems should be easily visible and adjustable to accommodate different cognitive levels and daily routines. A multi-disciplinary therapy center developed a modular magnetic scheduling system with interchangeable picture cards and text labels, allowing clients to physically move tokens representing completed activities.

Budget-friendly solutions include using clear pocket displays with printed cards or whiteboard panels with removable elements. For more sophisticated implementations, digital displays can be programmed to show personalized schedules with timing reminders. One particularly effective system used a combination of wall-mounted schedules for group activities and portable schedule books for individual sessions, allowing for both structure and flexibility.

Well-designed organization systems in transition spaces support independence and reduce anxiety by making resources easily accessible and activities predictable. Consider implementing clear storage solutions with visual labels combining pictures and text. A pediatric therapy facility created a "transition station" system where each client had a designated cubby with color-coded containers for different activities, making it easy to prepare for upcoming sessions.

For varying budgets, solutions range from simple labeled bins and hooks to custom-built storage walls with individual compartments. One innovative approach involved using transparent storage containers with LED lights that illuminated when it was time to access specific materials, helping clients with sequential processing challenges.

When designing transition spaces, consider these practical recommendations:

Install adequate lighting with adjustable brightness levels to accommodate different sensory sensitivities. Use consistent visual cues throughout the space to help with navigation and orientation. Create clear pathways with minimal obstacles, using flooring patterns or wall designs to naturally guide movement. Implement storage solutions at appropriate heights for different user groups, with clear labeling systems combining text, symbols, and colors.

From a therapeutic perspective, transition spaces should support emotional regulation and independence while promoting social awareness. Include elements that help individuals recognize and prepare for environmental changes, such as visual timers or countdown systems. Consider incorporating self-regulation tools like breathing guides mounted on walls or quiet corners for brief breaks.

A comprehensive rehabilitation center developed a "transition toolkit" system where clients could access personalized regulation items (stress balls, fidget tools, noise-canceling headphones) stored in easily accessible locations throughout transition spaces. This system supported self-advocacy and independence while maintaining organization.

Different individuals may require varying levels of sensory input during transitions. Design spaces with adjustable sensory features, such as dimmable lighting or sound-dampening options. For facilities on a budget, simple solutions like removable wall panels with different textures or portable sensory tools can be effective.

The success of transition spaces often depends on finding the right balance between structure and flexibility, allowing for personalization while maintaining clear organizational systems. Regular assessment and adjustment of these spaces ensure they continue to meet the evolving needs of users while supporting therapeutic goals.

20. Future Adaptability

Future Adaptability in therapeutic space design focuses on creating environments that can evolve alongside individuals' developing needs, abilities, and preferences. This forward-thinking approach ensures spaces remain functional and supportive while minimizing the need for costly renovations or complete overhauls as needs change over time. The concept encompasses several key areas that work together to create truly adaptable spaces.

Designing spaces that grow with children requires careful consideration of both current and anticipated future needs. The key lies in creating flexible foundations that can be easily modified without major structural changes. A family therapy center demonstrated this principle effectively by implementing an adjustable workstation system that transformed from toddler-height activity tables to teen-appropriate desk spaces through a series of simple hardware adjustments, serving clients from ages 2 to 18 without replacement. Height-adjustable elements throughout the space, including wall-mounted storage systems with adjustable shelving, allow for modification of storage heights and configurations as children grow. One innovative approach involved installing a "growth wall" with modular components that could be rearranged to accommodate changing needs – from low toy storage in early years to book shelves and desk space for older children.

Modular design principles enable spaces to be reconfigured quickly and efficiently as needs evolve. A notable example comes from a pediatric therapy room that utilized a custom-designed wall panel system where sensory elements, activity stations, and storage components could be easily swapped out or rearranged. The initial investment in the panel framework paid for itself within two years through reduced renovation costs. For budget-conscious implementations, furniture and storage solutions that can be easily recombined or repurposed have proven effective. Simple cube storage units can function as room dividers, seating, or display spaces depending on orientation and accessories. One particularly successful approach involved creating "activity pods" using mobile furniture elements that could be reconfigured for different therapeutic activities throughout the day.

Adaptable furniture solutions provide long-term value while accommodating changing needs. A school therapy department successfully implemented a furniture system where tables could be adjusted from individual workstations to group collaboration spaces, with height adjustability ranging from 12 to 30 inches. The system included removable privacy screens and interchangeable surface materials to support different activities. Solutions for various budgets range from basic adjustable-height furniture to sophisticated modular systems. Simple additions like furniture risers or removable table leaves can extend the useful life of existing pieces. One creative solution involved designing custom furniture covers that could be easily changed to update the aesthetic as children's preferences evolved, maintaining familiar and comfortable pieces while refreshing their appearance.

Long-term planning requires consideration of both physical and therapeutic needs over time. Spaces must be created that can accommodate different therapy modalities as treatment goals evolve. A private practice exemplified this approach by designing a convertible therapy space that could transition from early intervention services to teen counseling sessions through simple furniture rearrangement and accessory changes, serving clients throughout their developmental journey. Technology infrastructure planning proves essential, such as pre-wiring for potential electronic additions or installing adaptable mounting systems for therapeutic equipment. One successful approach involved creating a "future-ready" therapy room with modular wall panels that could accommodate various equipment configurations while maintaining a clean, organized appearance.

When implementing adaptable spaces, several practical considerations come into play. Storage systems should be adjustable without requiring professional assistance, and furniture should offer multiple configuration options to maximize space utility. Modular wall systems allow for easy updates to visual supports and therapeutic tools, while mobile storage solutions can be easily reorganized as needs change. For varying budgets, solutions can range from DIY modular systems using basic materials to professional-grade adjustable furniture. The key lies in selecting materials and designs that maintain their functionality while allowing for modifications over time.

From a therapeutic perspective, adaptable spaces should support evolving treatment goals while maintaining familiar elements that provide security and comfort. Features should be easily modified to match developing skills and interests while preserving successful therapeutic elements. A pediatric therapy center demonstrated this principle by developing a "therapeutic toolkit" system where treatment spaces could be quickly modified using interchangeable sensory elements, activity stations, and support tools. This system allowed therapists to adapt the environment to match clients' progress while maintaining consistent core elements.

Creating adaptable spaces doesn't always require significant financial investment. Multi-purpose furniture can serve different functions as needs change, and simple modular storage systems can be reconfigured easily. Movable dividers and portable equipment create flexible zones, while basic storage solutions can be modified using common tools. The success of future-adaptable spaces often depends on thorough initial planning and selecting versatile basic elements that can be modified over time. Regular assessment of space utilization and user needs helps inform timely adjustments and ensures the environment continues to support therapeutic goals effectively. Through careful consideration of these elements, spaces can be designed to grow and adapt alongside their users, providing consistent support throughout various developmental stages and therapeutic needs.

21. Community Resources

Community resources play a vital role in creating successful therapeutic environments, offering essential support networks that can transform abstract design concepts into practical realities. Understanding and accessing these resources requires a strategic approach that considers both immediate needs and long-term goals while remaining sensitive to various budget constraints and individual circumstances.

Professional support forms the foundation of successful therapeutic environment creation, with occupational therapists, physical therapists, and other healthcare professionals offering invaluable insights into specific design requirements. A notable example comes from a collaborative project in Portland, where a family worked with an occupational therapist who coordinated with local designers and contractors to create a sensory-friendly home renovation. The therapist's expertise helped translate clinical needs into practical design elements, while maintaining budget consciousness through strategic material selection and phased implementation. This project demonstrated how professional guidance can significantly improve outcomes while potentially reducing costs by avoiding expensive modifications later.

Finding qualified contractors who understand therapeutic design principles presents a unique challenge that requires careful consideration and thorough vetting. A successful past study from Minneapolis illustrates this process, where a support group for parents of children with sensory processing differences created a shared database of contractors experienced in therapeutic modifications. This resource proved invaluable as it included detailed reviews, project photos, and specific expertise areas. The contractors listed had demonstrated understanding of unique requirements such as specific lighting installations, sound dampening techniques, and safety modifications. Many of these professionals had pursued additional training in universal design and accessibility modifications, making them particularly valuable resources for families seeking specialized renovations.

Support groups serve as crucial information hubs and emotional support networks for families undertaking therapeutic environment modifications. An exemplary model exists in Chicago, where a monthly meeting combines practical workshops with peer support. These gatherings feature presentations from experienced parents, therapeutic professionals, and design experts, while also providing opportunities for resource sharing and problem-solving. The group maintains an online platform where members share vendor recommendations, design solutions, and cost-saving strategies. This combination of in-person and digital support has proven particularly effective in helping families navigate complex design decisions while staying within their budgets.

Financial assistance options, though sometimes challenging to navigate, can make therapeutic modifications accessible to families across various economic situations. A comprehensive approach to finding funding involves exploring multiple avenues simultaneously. For instance, a family in Boston successfully combined grants from three different sources: a local disability advocacy organization, a home modification program through their state's housing authority, and a specialized healthcare funding program. Their experience became a model for other families, demonstrating how layering different funding sources can make seemingly unattainable modifications possible. Many communities offer specific programs for therapeutic home modifications, though these resources often require persistent research and application efforts to access.

Local design professionals often provide valuable services through pro bono or reduced-fee programs specifically targeted at therapeutic environment creation. A remarkable initiative in Seattle pairs experienced designers with families requiring therapeutic modifications, offering initial consultations and basic design plans at no cost. These professionals help families prioritize modifications based on impact and budget, creating phased implementation plans that make larger projects manageable. The program has successfully served over fifty families, creating a valuable template for similar initiatives in other communities.

Educational resources play a crucial role in empowering families to make informed decisions about therapeutic environment modifications. Community colleges and vocational schools sometimes offer workshops on basic construction and design principles, which can help families better understand and manage smaller modification projects. A successful program in Atlanta provides monthly workshops covering topics from basic tool use to simple sensory room creation, helping families tackle some modifications independently while better understanding when professional help is necessary.

The integration of community resources requires careful coordination and often benefits from designated project management support. Some communities have developed volunteer coordinator positions specifically focused on helping families navigate available resources and create comprehensive project plans. These coordinators help match families with appropriate professionals, identify funding opportunities, and create realistic timelines for modifications. This coordinated approach has proven particularly effective in helping families maximize available resources while avoiding common pitfalls in the modification process.

Documentation and sharing of successful projects has become an increasingly important aspect of community resource utilization. Many support groups now maintain detailed past studies of completed projects, including budget breakdowns, timeline information, and lessons learned. These resources help subsequent families better understand the scope of potential projects and make more informed decisions about their own modifications. The sharing of both successes and challenges has created a valuable knowledge base that continues to grow and evolve as more families undertake therapeutic environment modifications.

www.ingramcontent.com/pod-product-compliance
Lightning Source LLC
Chambersburg PA
CBHW080638280726
48659CB00025BA/2560